SCROLL SAWING IN METAL:

PATTERNS AND TECHNIQUES

FRANK POZSGAI &
MARK DOWNING

Schiffer Publishing Ltd
80 Lower Valley Road, Atglen, PA 19310 USA

Dedication

To my entire family, with much thanks
for their love and support.
And a very special thanks to Mark Downing in collaborating
with us in producing this book.

Library of Congress Card Number: 2002100049

Designed by John P. Cheek
Cover design by Bruce M. Waters
Type set in Korinna BT/Korinna BT

ISBN: 0-7643-1564-1
Printed in China

Published by Schiffer Publishing Ltd.
4880 Lower Valley Road
Atglen, PA 19310
Phone: (610) 593-1777; Fax: (610) 593-2002
E-mail: Schifferbk@aol.com
Please visit our web site catalog at
www.schifferbooks.com
We are always looking for people to write books on new and related subjects. If you have an idea for a book please contact us at the above address.

This book may be purchased from the publisher.
Include $3.95 for shipping.
Please try your bookstore first.
You may write for a free catalog.

In Europe, Schiffer books are distributed by
Bushwood Books
6 Marksbury Ave.
Kew Gardens
Surrey TW9 4JF England
Phone: 44 (0) 20 8392-8585; Fax: 44 (0) 20 8392-9876
E-mail: Bushwd@aol.com
Free postage in the U.K., Europe; air mail at cost.

Contents

Acknowledgments

Many outstanding companies combined efforts to assist Pozsgai's Designs in making this book possible. Questions about equipment and accessories may be directed to: •Woodcrafters, Portland, Oregon; •Penn State Industries, Philadelphia, Pennsylvania; •The Olson Saw Co., Bethel, Connecticut; •The Woodworking Store, Hickey, North Carolina; •Porter Cable Delta Machinery, Jackson, Tennessee; •Wildwood Designs, Inc., Richland Center, Wisconsin; •Meisel Hardware Specialties, Mound, Minnesota; •Amana Tool Corp, Farmingdale, New York; Clackamas Steel & Mfg. Inc., Clackamas, Oregon; Alaskan Copper & Brass Co., Portland, Oregon; K&S Engineering Co., Chicago, Illinois.

My thanks goes out to all these fine companies and their helpful people.

Introduction

Scroll Sawing in Metal: Patterns & Techniques was designed to enhance one's ability to use their saws. It will delight both the beginner and advanced sawyer to see their accomplishment in working with these materials. All of these ornamental patterns are original size, however your craft is only limited by your imagination in how you choose to display them. There are numerous ways to utilize these patterns and techniques. One can be very creative.

Here are some ideas:

- Make pictures by adding a bracket and frame.
- Make a pen and pencil set by adding a simple base.
- Make clock sets by adding the popular 1-3/8" mini-clock insert.
- Make refrigerator mounts by adding a magnet.
- Make lamp shades and much more.
- Additional concepts include shelves, jewelry boxes, tissue dispensers, name signs, key holder racks, wastebaskets, and dresser drawer pulls.

Many of these ideas are illustrated on the following pages.

For the sake of all sawyer's we will be adding to any of our future books a complete scroll saw blades selection chart, as well as a general (SPM) blade guide. This information will be very beneficial in improving your knowledge with respect to proper blade selection.

Once again I would appreciate hearing from you about your success with these projects. And please send me any suggestions or requests for future pattern designs. "Happy cuttin' to ya!"

Instructions & Tips

Characteristics of Metals

Copper stock: A common reddish metallic element that is ductile and malleable. Electolytic Tough Pitch copper (ETP) has long been the standard type of commercial wrought copper to produce various items including sheet stock. The composition is copper (min.) 99.9% and oxygen (nom.) 0.04%. This copper sheet stock should be the material used by various crafters and sawyers.

Brass stock: An alloy consisting essentially of copper and zinc in variable proportions. Free milling engraver's brass sheet can be cut to enhance one's project. The composition of this brass is copper 62%, zinc 35.5%, lead 2.5%.

Steel stock: Cold rolled steel is another material which can be used. This stock typically consists of fourteen various alloys to create a low carbon sheet stock.

Other metals: The following materials are also useful in metal scroll saw work.

Shim brass: copper 70.0%, zinc 30.0%
Phosphor bronze: copper 94.75%, tin 5.0%, phosphorus 0.25%.
Silicon bronze: copper 95.8%, silicon 3.1%, manganese 1.1%
Aluminum bronze: copper 91.0%, aluminum 7.0%, iron 2,0%, zinc 0.2%
Naval bronze: copper 60.0%, zinc 39.25%, tin 0.75%
Aluminum (3003): manganese 1.2%, aluminum 98.8%
Aluminum (6061): manganese 1.0%, silicon 0.06%, chromium 0.25%, copper 0.25%, aluminum 98.4%

While the primary materials used in this book are metals, one can also use plastics and leather to complement a particular project or enhance the presentation of a design.

Note: As a rule of thumb, a piece of soft metal up to 1/8" thick can be cut quite easily, whether one chooses to cut a single sheet of stock or several thinner sheets in a stack cut.

Metals Conversion Table

Decimal Equiv.	Approx. Gauge	Approx. Fraction	Aaprox. Millimeter
.022	24		0.59
.025	23		0.64
.028	22		0.71
.032	21	1/32"	0.81
.035	20		0.89
.042	19		1.07
.049	18		1.24
.054	17		1.37
.065	16	1/16"	1.65
.072	15		1.83
.083	14		2.11
.095	13	3/32"	2.41
.109	12		2.77
.120	11		3.05
.125		1/8"	3.18
.134	10		3.40
.148	9		3.76
.156	8	5/32"	3.96
.180	7		4.57
.188		3/16"	4.76
.203	6		5.56
.219	5	7/32"	5.56
.238	4		6.05
.250		1/4"	6.35
.259	3		6.58
.281	2	9/32"	7.14
.300	1		7.62
.313		5/16"	7.94
.344		11/32"	8.74
.375		3/8"	9.53
.380			9.65
.406		13/32"	10.31
.425			10.80
.438		7/16"	11.13
.454			11.53
.469		15/32"	11.91
.500		1/2"	12.70
.563		9/16"	14.30
.625		5/8"	15.88
.688		11/16"	17.48
.750		3/4"	19.05
.813		13.16"	20.65
.875		7/8"	22.23
.938		15/16"	23.83
1.00		1"	25.40

Sourcing Your Materials

With the aid of computers and an access to the internet there is nothing one can't find. However, if one does not have access, your yellow pages are sure to direct you to these items. Typically you local hardware stores have the materials mentioned in stock or can order them for you.

Usually you can buy cold rolled steel, copper, and aluminum sheet from a local sheet metal shop, usually as scrap at scrap prices. For copper sheet pieces of approximately 16 ounces per square foot, expect to pay 10 to 12 cents an ounce. Sometimes they just give you the cold rolled steel scrap cut-offs for free. Of course, it helps to give them something nice from your shop occasionally.

Sheet metal shops are more than willing to sell you "new" sheet metal in full sheets, usually 4 feet by 10 feet. They will also shear the full sheets into more manageable pieces with the added labor charge, usually reasonable. I pay $30 to $40 for a full 4' x 10' piece of 24 gauge cold rolled steel, depending on the cutting fee. Also a brief note, K&S Engineering Co. of Chicago, Illinois manufactures and sells metal products. Tap Plastics, Inc. of Dublin, California can provide you various plastics.

Special Cutting Hints

- The blade you use should have a minimum of three teeth per material thickness

- When cutting metal you can cut at the same speed and intricacy that you would cut any other material. Be careful of too much forward pressure when cutting, as this will cause the blade to prematurely break.

  Note: As an example, when I cut two sheets of 24 gauge steel or two sheets of copper in 16 to 20 ounce size, I cut at the highest cutting speed. However, when I cut three sheets of either of these metals, reducing the cutting speed in half works best.

- If you set up and cut for marquetry panels, you need to keep in mind that you cannot "waste" cut into the background or drill any pilot holes that are not in a sharp turn area of the design.

- Use 2" clear 3-M packing tape to envelop your project several times. When cutting the tape continually lubricates the scroll saw blade.

The Right Blade for the Right Job

Contrary to numerous opinions, just like mine, it's the end result of what one achieves with the scroll saw that counts. I am repeatedly asked "what blade should I use?" There are too many variables to consider to give a pat answer to that question! The saw itself whether it's an Excalibur, a Hegner, Delta, RBI Hawk, or an import, is not the most important factor. Most saws can be made to do a good job. More important factors are the blade tension, the feed rate, your sensitivity, the speed (SPM), and the type of material you are cutting.

That being said, the blade is the single most important component of a scroll saw! If the right blade is not used for the job, the results won't be worth anything. And there are so many variables that you need to have a variety of blades available for your saw. Remember that one or two common blades will not be enough for a novice, much less the accomplished scroller.

Choosing the correct blade size and tooth style for the material to be cut is the key factor for accurate and smooth scroll sawing. If it is done right, one can eliminate or reduce the constant problem of sanding! Also, much to everyone's surprise, in cutting metals the standard skip tooth fret blades seem to outperform the traditional metal cutting scroll saw blades. You may use any skip tooth blade up through a #5 easily, however, I prefer to use size 2/0 to #2 blades for inside cuts and cutting marquetry panels. You will use more blades, so buy your blades by the gross.

OLSON®

Scroll Saw Blades

Selection Chart

Material: Hard Wood 1/2"–3/4", Hard Wood to 1½", Soft Wood to 1/2"–3/4", Soft Wood to 1½", Veneer/Thin Wood to 3/16", Plywood, MDF, Particle Board, Corian 1/8"–1/2", Plastic 1/2"–3/4", Non Ferrous Metal, Aluminum

Finish: Smooth, Splinter-Free, Medium

Recommended / Can Use / Not Recommended

Olson No.	Univ. No.	Width	Thickness	TPI/ No. Rev.	Tooth Style	Pilot Hole	Application	Corian	Plastic
PGT® Precision Ground Tooth (The Best!)							Skip Tooth PGT / Double Tooth PGT		
455RG	5RG	.045"	.018"	12/9	Skip	1/16"	Ultra smooth finish, straight or close radius cutting, splinter-free, clean edges	1/8"	1/8"
457RG	7RG	.047"	.018"	10/7	Skip	1/16"		3/8"	3/8"
459RG	9RG	.049"	.018"	8/6	Skip	1/16"		1/2"	3/4"
495RG	5RG	.045"	.018"	12/8	Double	1/16"		1/8"	1/8"
497RG	7RG	.047"	.018"	10.5/8	Double	1/16"		3/8"	3/8"
499RG	9RG	.049"	.018"	9/6	Double	1/16"		1/2"	3/4"
Crown Tooth™									
620	2/0	.024"	.011"	20	Crown	1/32"	Veining, line art, extreme radius cutting	1/8"	1/8"
622	2	.026"	.013"	20	Crown	3/64"	Extreme radius, delicate fretwork	1/8"	1/8"
623	3	.032"	.014"	16	Crown	3/64"	Tight radius fretwork	1/8"	3/16"
625	5	.038"	.016"	16	Crown	1/16"	Close radius fretwork, general purpose	1/8"	1/4"
627	7	.045"	.017"	11	Crown	1/16"	Close radius, general purpose	1/8"	3/4"
629	9	.053"	.018"	6	Crown	1/16"	General purpose, multi-layers	1/8"	3/4"
632	12	.065"	.024"	6	Crown	5/64"	Heavy duty for faster cuts	1/2"	3/4"
Reverse Tooth									
440R	2/0	.022"	.010"	28/21	Skip	1/32"	Veining, line art, extreme radius cutting		
443R	2R	.029"	.012"	20/14	Skip	3/64"	Extreme radius, delicate fretwork		
446R	5R	.038"	.016"	12.5/9	Skip	3/64"	Close radius fretwork, general purpose		
448R	7R	.047"	.017"	11.5/8	Skip	1/16"	Close radius, general purpose		
450R	9R	.054"	.019"	11.5/8	Skip	1/16"	General purpose, multi-layers		
453R	12R	.062"	.024"	9.5/6	Skip	5/64"	Heavy duty for faster cuts		
420R	–	.100"	.022"	9/5	Skip	1/8"	For cutting thick wood and multi-layers		
Flat End Spiral									
468	2	–	.035"	41	–	5/64"	Medium speed and medium finish of hard and soft wood, plaster, and wallboard		
469	4	–	.041"	36	–	7/64"			
Spiral									
461	0	–	.032"	46	–	3/64"	Bevel cut letters, etc., medium finish fretwork and workpieces too large to turn		
463	2	–	.035"	41	–	5/64"			
465	4	–	.041"	36	–	7/64"			

PGT® blades have razor sharp reverse teeth with widely spaced gullets for cutting straighter, faster, smoother, more accurately. PGT's minimize burning and provide the ultimate sand-free, splinterless finish with a clean edge. Double tooth style is especially good for cutting hard woods.

Hint! Reverse Tooth blades work best with 1-2 reverse teeth showing above the table on the upstroke! Adjust blade in holder or trim when necessary.

Unique **Crown Tooth** blades cut on both up and down strokes. Two way cutting action provides a smooth, splinterless finish, and clean edges. When worn, the blade can be turned over for cutting with a fresh set of teeth!

Hint! Tension blade properly! With reasonable force the center of the blade should not move more than 1/8" front to back. Too little tension weakens performance.

Reverse Tooth blades have skip style teeth and reverse teeth that eliminate underside tearout and provide a smooth, splinterless finish.

Hint! More teeth per inch provide a finer cut (good for soft wood). Less TPI provide a coarser cut (good for hard wood). Use the highest number blade for your application (larger blades are more durable).

Flat End Spiral blades are the same as our regular spiral blades, but with flat ends for easier blade installation and retention. Offered in the two most popular sizes.

Spiral blades saw in all directions with 360° cutting capability. Excellent for 0° radius scroll/fret work – no need to turn the workpiece. Bevel cut letters and numbers.

The Olson Saw Company, Bethel, CT 06801 USA

OL-1052 n 5/00

Courtesy Olson Saw Co.

OLSON®

Scroll Saw Blades

Selection Chart

Material: Hard Wood 1/2″ – 3/4″ · Hard Wood to 1½″ · Soft Wood to 1/2″ – 3/4″ · Soft Wood to 1½″ · Veneer/Thin Wood to 3/16″ · Plywood · MDF · Particle Board · Corian 1/8″ – 1/2″ · Plastic 1/2″ – 3/4″ · Non Ferrous Metal · Aluminum

Finish: Smooth · Splinter-Free · Medium

Recommended · Can Use · Not Recommended

Olson No.	Univ. No.	Width	Thickness	TPI/ No. Rev.	Tooth Style	Pilot Hole	Application
Thick Wood							
408	–	.080″	.018″	7	Hook	3/32″	Thick wood – up to 2″ without burning!
Skip Tooth							
400	3/0	.022″	.008″	33	Skip	1/32″	Ultra intricate sawing, veining, line art, close knit jig saw puzzles
440	2/0	.022″	.010″	28	Skip	1/32″	Extremely intricate sawing, veining, line art
443	2	.029″	.012″	20	Skip	3/64″	Tight radius work, fretwork
445	4	.035″	.015″	15	Skip	1/16″	Tight radius work, fretwork
446	5	.038″	.016″	12.5	Skip	1/16″	Close radius cutting
448	7	.045″	.017″	11.5	Skip	1/16″	General Purpose
450	9	.053″	.018″	11.5	Skip	1/16″	General Purpose
453	12	.062″	.024″	9.5	Skip	5/64″	Heavy duty for fast cuts
Pinned							
424P	–	.070″	.010″	18.5	Skip	3/16″	Skip style teeth/ Very thin cuts
405P	–	.110″	.018″	20	Reg.	3/16″	Regular style teeth/ thin cuts
410P	–	.100″	.018″	7	Hook	3/16″	Thick wood, up to 2″ without burning!
411P	–	.110″	.018″	15	Reg.	3/16″	General purpose, regular style teeth
412P	–	.110″	.018″	10	Reg.	3/16″	Regular style teeth, fast cutting
420RP	–	.110″	.018″	9/5	Skip	3/16″	Heavy duty widely-spaced set teeth for fast cutting
Double Tooth							
432	3/0	.023″	.008″	33	Dbl.	1/32″	Ultra intricate sawing, veining, line art, close knit jig saw puzzles
433	2/0	.023″	.011″	37	Dbl.	1/32″	Veining, line art & marquetry
434	1	.026″	.013″	30	Dbl.	3/64″	Delicate fretwork
435	3	.032″	.014″	23	Dbl.	3/64″	Extremely intricate sawing
436	5	.038″	.016″	16	Dbl.	1/16″	Tight radius work
437	7	.044″	.018″	13	Dbl.	1/16″	Close radius cutting
438	9	.053″	.018″	11	Dbl.	1/16″	General purpose
439	12	.061″	.022″	10	Dbl.	5/64″	Heavy duty, fast cuts
Metal Cutting							
485	–	.041″	.019″	30	Reg.	–	Very thin metal sheets
487	–	.049″	.022″	25	Reg.	–	Thin metal sheets
490	–	.070″	.023″	20	Reg.	–	Thicker metal sheets

Hint! (All Blades) For best performance, use lower numbers for thinner stock and higher numbers for thicker stock.

Skip tooth blades are excellent for fast cuts that provide smooth finishes and good chip clearance.

Hint! (All Blades) For best performance, use lower numbers for tighter radii and higher numbers for more general purpose cuts.

Pinned scroll saw blades are for machines that require 5″ pinned blades. They are perfect for Sears Craftsman, Penn State, Delta, Ryobi and all 15″ and 16″ imported scroll saws that require pinned blades.

Hint! Slow feed rate down! Relax! Let the blade do the cutting to minimize burning. Also, use a lube stick on the blade or clear shipping tape on the workpiece to inhibit scorching.

Double tooth blades have two teeth together followed by a flat space for efficient chip removal. They cut fast, leaving clean edges in wood and plastic.

Metal cutting blades have more teeth per inch required for cutting thin metal and other hard materials.

The Olson Saw Company, Bethel, CT 06801 USA

OL-1052 n 5/00

Courtesy Olson Saw Co.

Scroll Saw Cutting Preparations

- **Wax the work table** periodically. This will help the stock slide easily over the work table for better control.

- **Level the table**, and, using a square, check to see if the blade is at an angle of 90 degrees or perpendicular to the saw table.

- **Select the blade**. Remember, use the right blade for the right material. For guidance, check out the blade use Guideline Chart in this book.

- **Check blade tension.** The Rule of Thumb: When you push the blade front to back with your thumb, you should get a 1/8" deflection. Remember periodically blade tension adjustment is a must.

- **Decide on a cutting speed.** Establish the proper "SPM," Strokes Per Minute, for the project. Check out the General Guide to Cutting Speed for the materials you have selected. Remember to read the section pertaining to special blade and cutting hints; as well as the right blade for the right job, To some sawyers this will truly be helpful.

- **Don't be afraid.** Learn not to be afraid of the scroll saw blade and work from 1/2" to 1" around the scroll saw blade while you are cutting. This is most important, and will make a BIG difference on your finish product.

Maintenance & Upkeep of your Scroll Saw

All scroll saws require periodic maintenance. This includes:

- Greasing (not oiling) of pivot bolts every 50-75 hours of running time. Note: On the new delta P-20 you have no choice but to oil.

- Checking your motor brushes periodically and replacing them as needed.

- Visually checking belts and or other wearing parts.

- Waxing the work table frequently.

- Cleaning the scroll saw periodically, especially around the motor & electronic controls. Compressed air works well for this task.

Safety Procedures

Read your owners operating manual is essential for all sawyers. Once again take care and truly enjoy your scroll saw.

Sizing, Copying, & Transferring the Pattern

- **Sizing & Copying the Pattern:** Use a photocopier to make several copies of the particular pattern you wish to cut out. Modify them to your satisfaction, by either enlarging them or reducing them to suit your needs. Your local copy stores also have a proportional scale on their photocopiers, if you wish to use them to scale your patterns.

- **Cut the pattern straight along the base.** This is important for proper alignment with the wood. If the bottom of the pattern is straight, it can be laid against the straight edge of the wood to give you a clean line for joining to a base later. The rest of the pattern can be cut roughly, outside the lines.

- **Transferring the Pattern to the Work Piece.** There are several products on the market one can choose to adhere the pattern to the work piece. They include: Glue Stic™ by Avery, 3M's Scotchbrand™ spray adhesive, rubber cement, etc. Make sure they are the repositionable or temporary bond items.

Selection of Materials

The provided patterns may be sawed from a wide variety of different materials & different thickness—the choices are entirely yours. The range can include wood products, plastic, or even metals.

However, as previously indicated, stay with the 1/8" thickness limit using various soft metals.

Note: In order to cut metal with a scroll saw using a standard skip tooth blade versus metal cutting scroll saw blades, you need to sandwich the metal between plywood. If you don't, the scroll saw blade will catch and slam the metal up and down on the scroll saw table, breaking the blade. Using this method enables one to cut more intricate designs much faster. If you were to try to do a fast turn with a metal cutting blade, it would more often than not break immediately.

General Characteristic & Manufacturing Processes of Scroll Saw Blades

•Material:	Carbon: .070%-.079% Silicone: 0.10%-.030% Manganese: 0.30%-0.70% Chromium: 0.10%
•Hardness:	RC 53-55
•Style (skip tooth):	15.0 TPI
•Dimension (tooth cut):	.001"/.008"
•Bend Test:	The Reverse Tooth Fret saw blade must be able to revolve around a 360° pin without fracturing. Then the blade must return to its relaxed state and remain bent.

All the carbon steel wire product produced in the U.S. today either comes from an open hearth or electric furnaces. The typical USA Acid Bessemer Process is what produces the superior quality grades of steel. Virtually all scroll saw and similar blades are manufactured from a non-resulphurized high carbon steel.

- Scroll Blades Regular Style Teeth (5"or6"): Blades are notched & set.
- Skip Tooth Fret, Saw Blades (5"): Blades are milled with no set.
- Reverse Skip Tooth Saw Blades (5"): Blades are milled with no set.
- Double Tooth Fret Saw Blades (5")—Blades are milled with no set.
- Metal Cutting Saw Blades (5"): Blades are milled with no set.
- Spiral Saw Blades (5"): Blades are milled with no set.
- PGT Saw Blades (5"): Blades are precision ground with no set.
- Double Tooth PGT Saw Blades (5"): Blades are precision ground with no set.
- Thick wood Saw Blades (5"): Blades are notched and set.

Note: for the experts out there NOTCHED BLADES are extremely sharp and can be equal to a milled or precision ground tooth blade.

Cutting Speed (SPM)

	APPLICATION	SPEED (SPM)
SOFT WOODS	High speed quickly & easily cuts pines, balsa wood, bass wood, plywood, cedar, fir and others	1600-2000
HARDWOODS	For making intricate cuts on cherry, walnut, oak, teak, ash, maple, purple heart, rosewood and others without burning wood. With stock that is 3/4" & above use the 3M tape trick.	1400-2000
METALS	Slow speed keeps blades cool to minimize breakage. Can cut brass, copper, aluminum, soft 16 to 20 gauge low carbine steel sheet stock and others, especially with skiptooth blades	400-700
PLASTICS	Slow speed helps to prevent melting of some cast acrylic, ASB, lexan & Plexiglas. Note: An extruded acrylic can be cut easily at 1500-1700 SPM	300-1000

The Project

Preparation and sequential steps for setting up and cutting metal cut-outs with a scroll saw.

Decide what kinds of metal you want to cut and whether you are setting up for just cut-outs, stencils, or marquetry panels. I usually set up with one of the following combinations:

- two sheets of 16 or 20 ounce copper, or
- two sheets of 24 gauge steel, or
- two sheets of 16 or 20 ounce copper and one sheet of 24 gauge steel, or
- two sheets of 24 gauge steel and one sheet of 16 or 20 ounce copper.

This last combination is the one I have selected for our project.

I also use combinations of steel, copper, aluminum, and brass, and often insert other materials between the sheets of metal, including leather, fabric, and hand made paper. Don't be afraid to experiment on your own!

I usually set up with the intention of cutting out marquetry panels. That way, I will end up with great stencils if I decide just to use the cut-outs. You need to do set ups in such a way that there will be very little vibration when cutting. For both of these reasons, your sheet metal needs to be in good condition. It should lie flat with no bends or dents.

Wipe the film of oil off of the sheet metal with a clean, dry cloth.

Cut the pieces of metal and the plywood that will hold it into the sizes you will need for the project.

Note: One of the best ways to cut metals to size is with the scroll saw. Place your selected metals between two pieces of plywood, one 1/4" thick and one 1/8" thick.

Clamp the wood-metal sandwich together .

Tightly and securely tape with 3-M Clear Plastic Tape. First go lengthwise...

then across.

The sandwich of wood should be completely wrapped in tape.

Use a #5 or a FR446 skip tooth blade in your saw. **Don't** use a bandsaw to cut your material because it tends to leave a large burr on the bottom of the cut.

Carefully cut the wood-metal sandwich to size.

The uncut sides of the tape should hold the package together until you are finished.

The result is metal and wood that are all identically and correctly cut.

I usually use Elmer's School Glue Gel between the pieces of metal (but not between the metal and the plywood) for the final cut. If you do the cutting soon after setting up, while the glue is wet and sticky, it will help reduce vibration and lubricate the blade somewhat. It will also reduce the chance of separation while the delicate cuts are being made. The glue should be washed off of the metal cut-outs with warm water as soon as you are finished cutting them out. (Leaving the glue on the metal too long will cause the metal to rust or oxidize.) I find that a bristle brush helps in washing the glue off. If you do not wash the glue off with water, you may sand it off after the glue has completely dried. (This often leaves small hairs of glue hanging off the edges of the cut out that are aggravating to remove.

Instead of glue, you may place sheets of wax paper between the sheets of metal and plywood to help lubricate the blade.

Apply the glue from the bottle.

Spread it out with a brush or rag...

to get an uniform coverage over the surface.

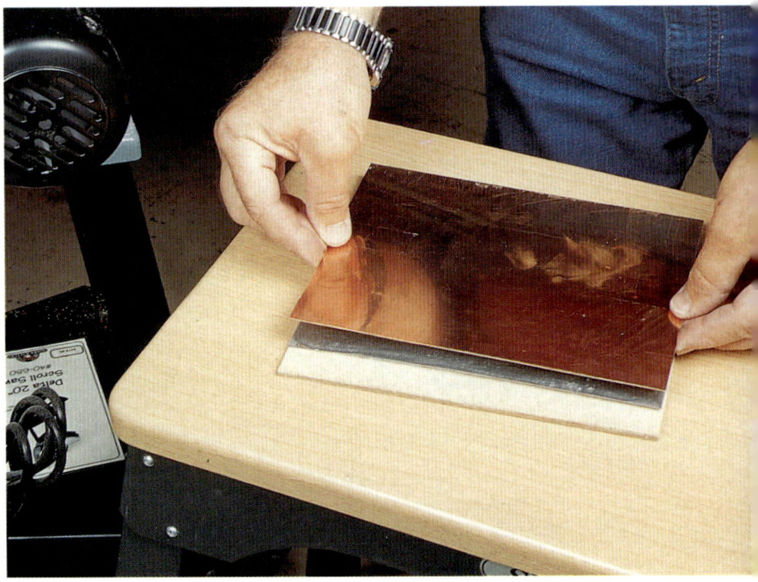

Join the next piece of metal and repeat the process.

When all the pieces are glued, put something heavy on the top so the sheets will stay pressed closely together until the glue firms up. Generally 1 to 3 minutes is more than ample time for Glue Gel to work.

Sandwich the glued sheets of metal between the two pieces of plywood, 1/4" and 1/8". Place the 1/4" piece of plywood on top when you cut. This will lessen the flexing and vibration.

The result.

Clamp the assembly together...

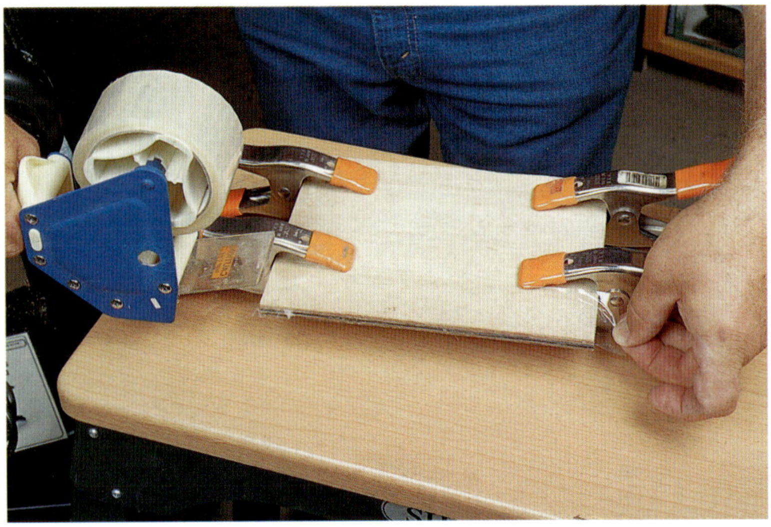

then wrap it completely with 3M clear plastic tape. You should wrap the set-up both crosswise and lengthwise with several layers of the tape. This will help keep the plywood and sheet metal from vibrating, and will also lubricate the blade while cutting.

The wrapped plywood/metal assembly.

Spray the bottom side of the paper design or pattern with spray adhesive.

Cut excess paper from around the design, but do not cut down to the lines.

Place on the top of the set-up. (Remember, the top is the 1/4" piece of plywood.)

For pilot holes, use a drill bit that is only large enough to allow the blade that you will be using to barely fit through the pilot hole. Since we will be cutting our project with a number 2/0 scrollsaw blade with a width of .022", we should use a number 68 drill bit which is .031" in diameter.

Whenever possible the pilot holes should go in a "sharp turn" area of the design or where two lines meet at 90 degrees or less. Do one hole for the outside line of the design...

and as many as necessary for the inside cuts.

Thread the blade through the pilot hole.

Usually I set the scroll saw table at a slight 3 degree angle. When doing this however, you must be sure to cut in the same direction all the time. You will find that you cut better and with smoother flow of the lines, cutting in one direction, either clockwise or counterclockwise.

The advantage of the angled cut is that it allows the cut pieces to fit into each other with a minimum of kerf showing. This cutting and reassembling of the cutouts and backgrounds is called marquetry. Do not angle the table if you are setting up to make cut outs and not marquetry panels.

Note: If you set up and cut for marquetry panels, you need to keep in mind that you cannot "waste" cut into the background or drill any pilot holes that are not in a sharp turn area of the design.

If all goes well the tape and the paper pattern should lift up like this.

After you are finished cutting, remove the plastic wrap from the plywood and separate the metal cutouts and backgrounds with a thin knife, spatula, or putty knife.

Here is the cut as seen in the plywood cover.

With careful cutting you end up with a marquetry panels or metal and wood cut-outs.

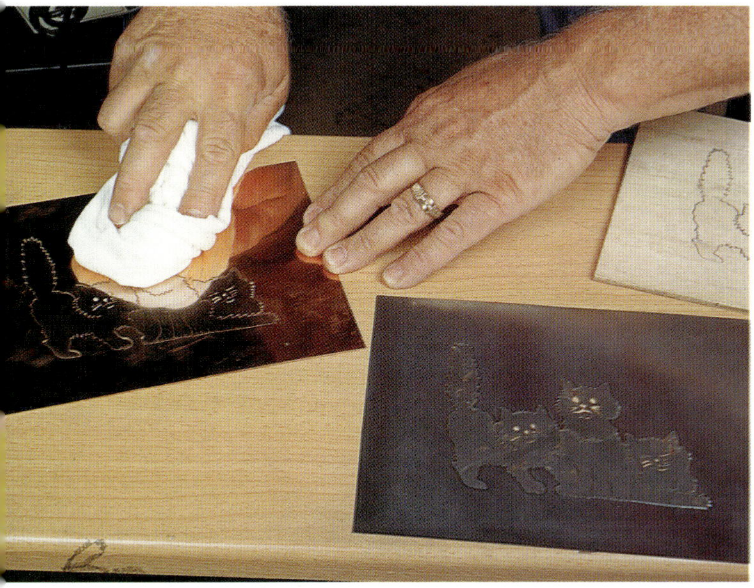

Carefully clean off any excess glue.

To assemble the marquetry panels, switch the background and cutouts. For example, insert a copper cutout into a steel background ...

...or a steel cutout into a copper background.

Note: the metal pieces of the marquetry panel should now be sanded and finished, either with chemical oxidation or heat patination. For chemical oxidation, sand the metal with 220 grit paper. For heat patination, sanding up through 600 grit will look much nicer.

I usually assemble the marquetry panel on a 1/4 inch piece of plywood the same size as the background. Sometimes I mount "sticky back" silver- or gold-colored foil on the 1/4" plywood.

Placing the foil behind the marquetry design will look good if you are not able or do not want to save the small inside cuts, or if you use the inside cutout and want the eyes, accent lines, and small cuts to be accented. You should be able to get other colors of foil or paper that would work as well. Try a local art supply, craft, or office supply store. Fabric, leather, and other metals will work in the same way.

To add texture to the background go over it with fine sand paper, sanding one way...

then the other.

The result.

Basic Finishing Tips

There are numerous ways to finish your project depending on the pattern you choose and type of metal you use, and including what style you want to present it. They include natural finishes, stains, paints, lacquers, and patinating, which is also called "verdigris" of your metal projects. In this process one would use an acetic-acid bath to oxidize the surface of the shiny metal, like copper, brass, or bronze. The visual effect of this process leaves a beautiful bluish-green deposit on copper making your project look awesome.

Remember, the choice is strictly a matter of personal preference. Another method one can choose is heat patinating, achieving similar results with different colors than those above. The finishing should be done first, before assembling and gluing a marquetry panel.

There are several ways to add patination to the piece. One is to simply heat it. On a fireproof surface, use a blowtorch or other high heat source to bring the piece to a high temperature. You will see the colors change as oxidation and other chemical changes take place. When you get something you like, stop and let the piece cool. Note that on most metals heat produces a more subdued patina on the back side, compared to the side where the direct flame was applied.

Note: a slow heating with a propane torch will let you observe the changes in colors. It will take practice to heat the metal just right and then stop to keep the color you want.

The result.

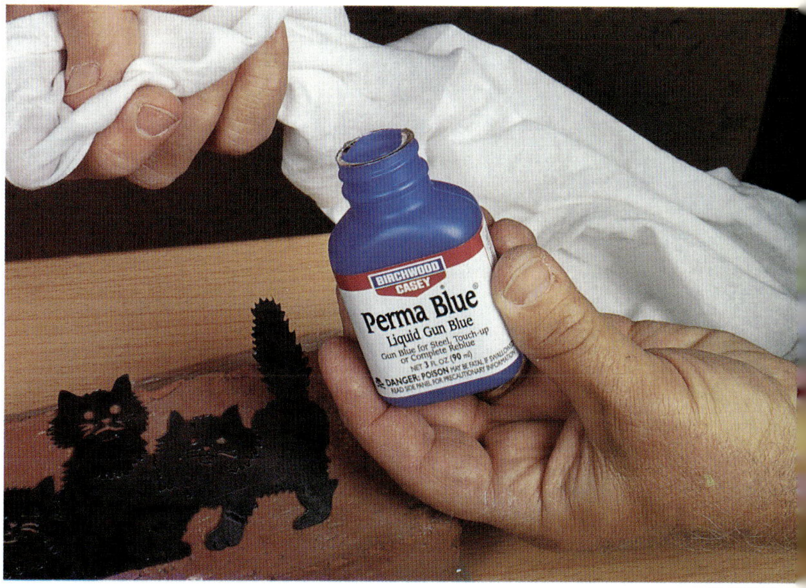

Chemicals, like this bluing agent, are also available.

Apply them to the piece, following the manufacturer's instructions. When I patinate the metal cutouts to stand alone, I use the chemical on both sides at once and then hang the piece with a thin piece of wire in a dark, enclosed place. This type of atmosphere seems to stabilize the patinating process and usually takes approximately 30 minutes for the metal to dry.

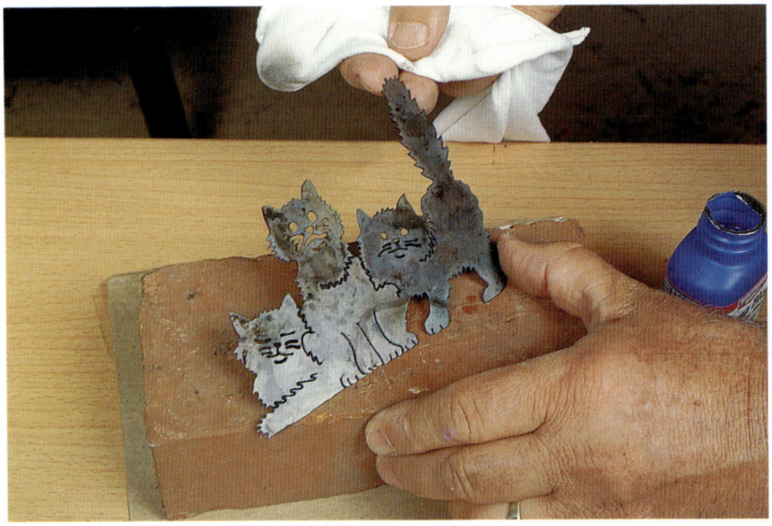

The result.

I usually use carpet tape to hold things together. Apply it to the back of the background piece.

To prevent unwanted oxidation carefully spray the piece with a clear lacquer. Avoid drips or bubbles.

Peel off the backing of the tape...

Decide on the assembly of the marquetry piece. I am using the patinated copper figure in the brushed steel background and placing on the gold foil board.

and stick the background to the foil-covered board.

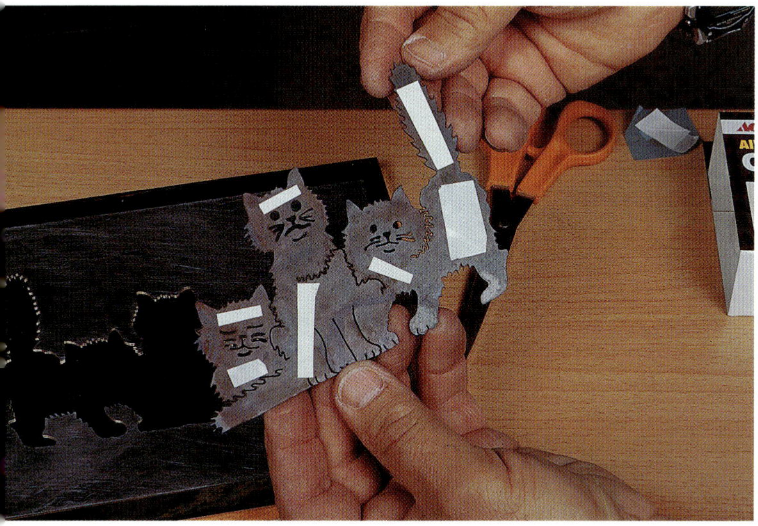

Carefully apply carpet tape to the copper central figure. Be certain it doesn't show through the holes.

Press the central figure in place.

Except for the frame the assembly is complete

As a final touch, I took stripes of copper and worked them around the edges for a frame.

Another Method of Assembly

You may assemble the marquetry panel upside down on a piece of "low tack" paper (such as air brush mask paper that you can obtain at an art supply store). Remember, the finished side of the metal goes down on the sticky side of the paper.

After the marquetry panel is assembled upside down on the low tack paper, you may spray or brush a good coat of contact glue. Then spray or brush another coat of glue on the surface you will use for the base. (I usually use a piece of 1/4 inch plywood that is 1/2 inch larger on all four sides) Be sure to allow the contact glue to dry thoroughly but remain tacky before joining the two pieces. If the glue is not dry enough, it may leak up through the joints of the panel. You may use construction grade contact glue or 3M 90 Hi Strength Spray contact glue, both of which should be available at any hardware store.

With the glued base lying on a flat surface, glue side up, carefully turn the assembled marquetry panel over so the glued side is down. Place the marquetry panel on the glued base. You must be sure you are aligned right the first time because as soon as the two glued surfaces touch, they are joined. It would be difficult to pull them apart for repositioning.

You may then place a thicker piece of plywood over the panel with a weight on top to press the panel to the base. (Remember that this can cause the glue to seep up through the pieces of the panel, especially if the contact glue was not dry enough.)

After the panel has dried overnight, cut the excess plywood from around the panel. You may wish to set your scroll saw table to a rather sharp angle for this. That way, the edge of the wood base will not show so much if you decide to hang the panel without framing it.

The Gallery

Lamps and Electrical Fixtures

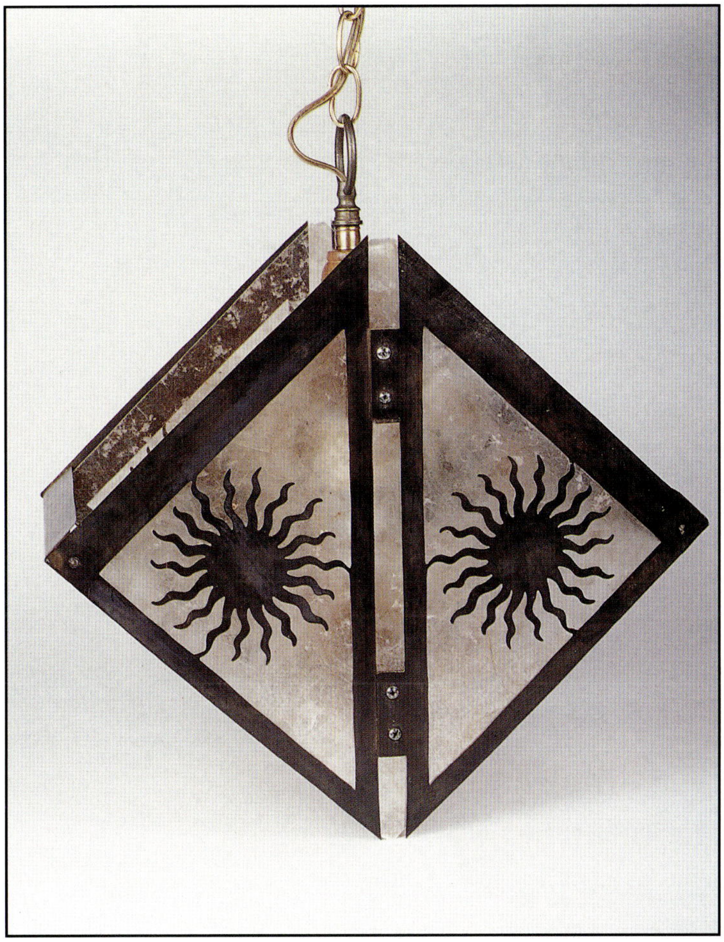

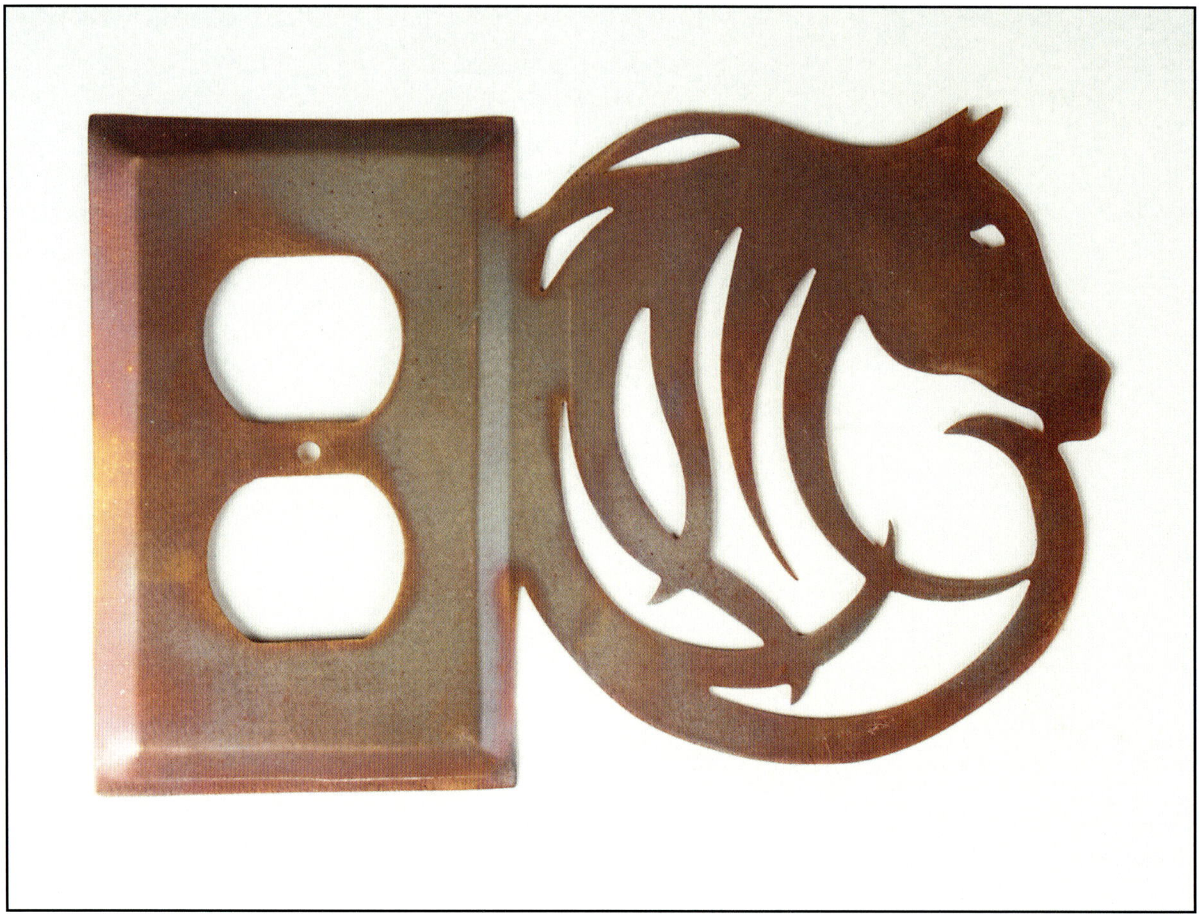

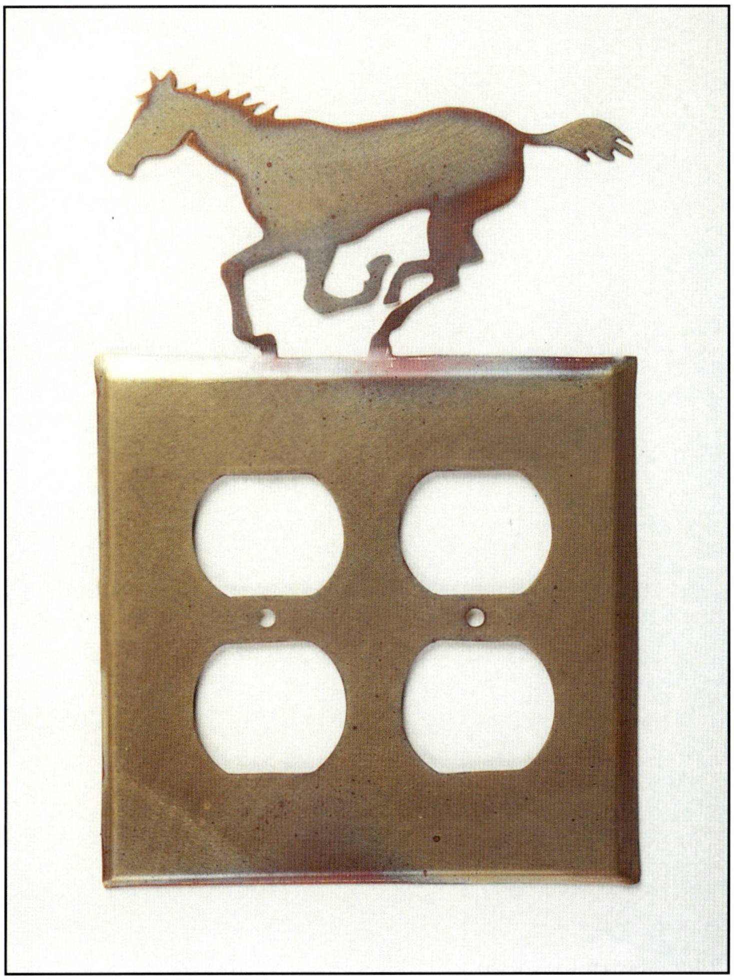

Earrings

Shelves

Drawer Pulls

Patterns

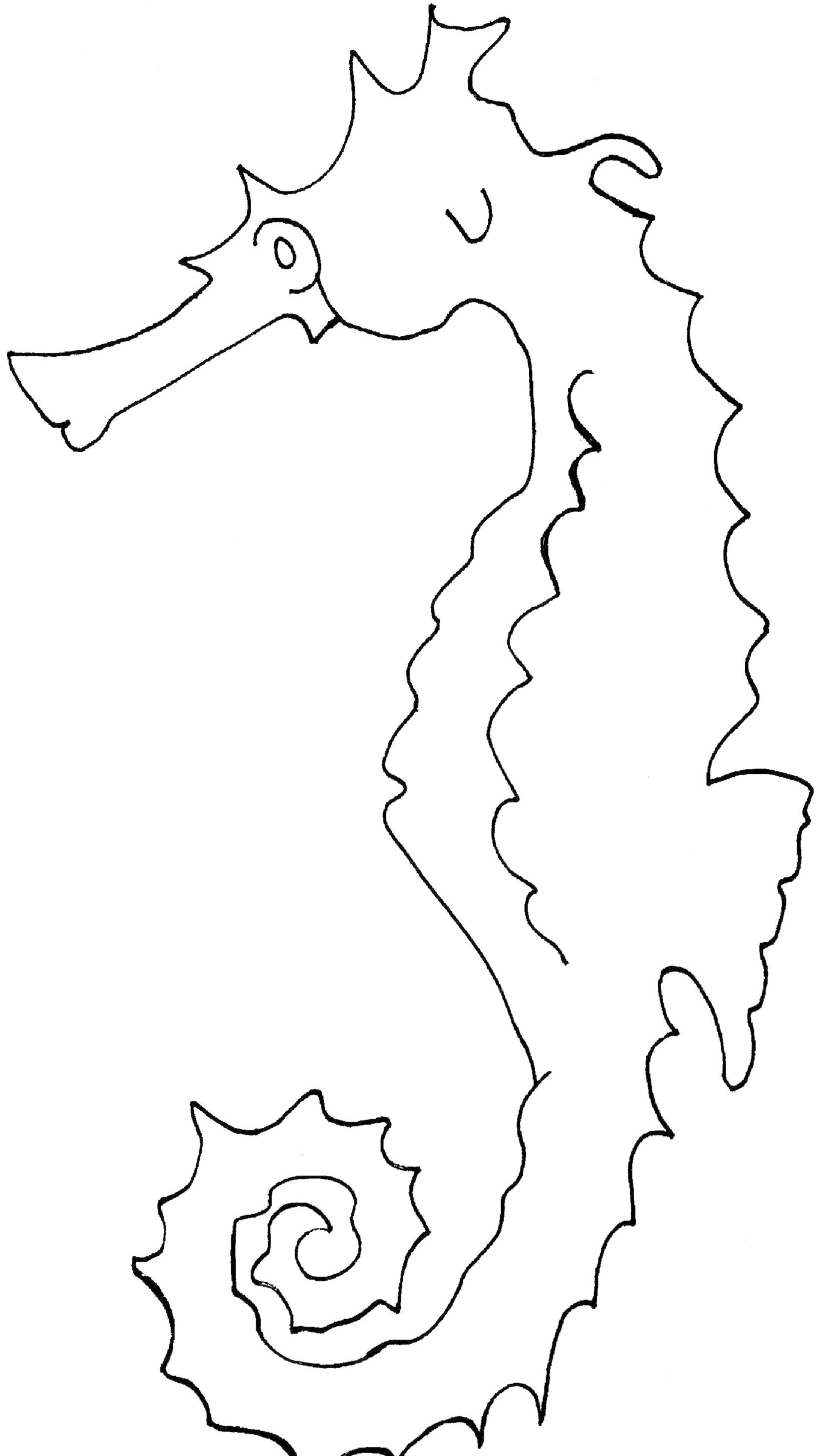

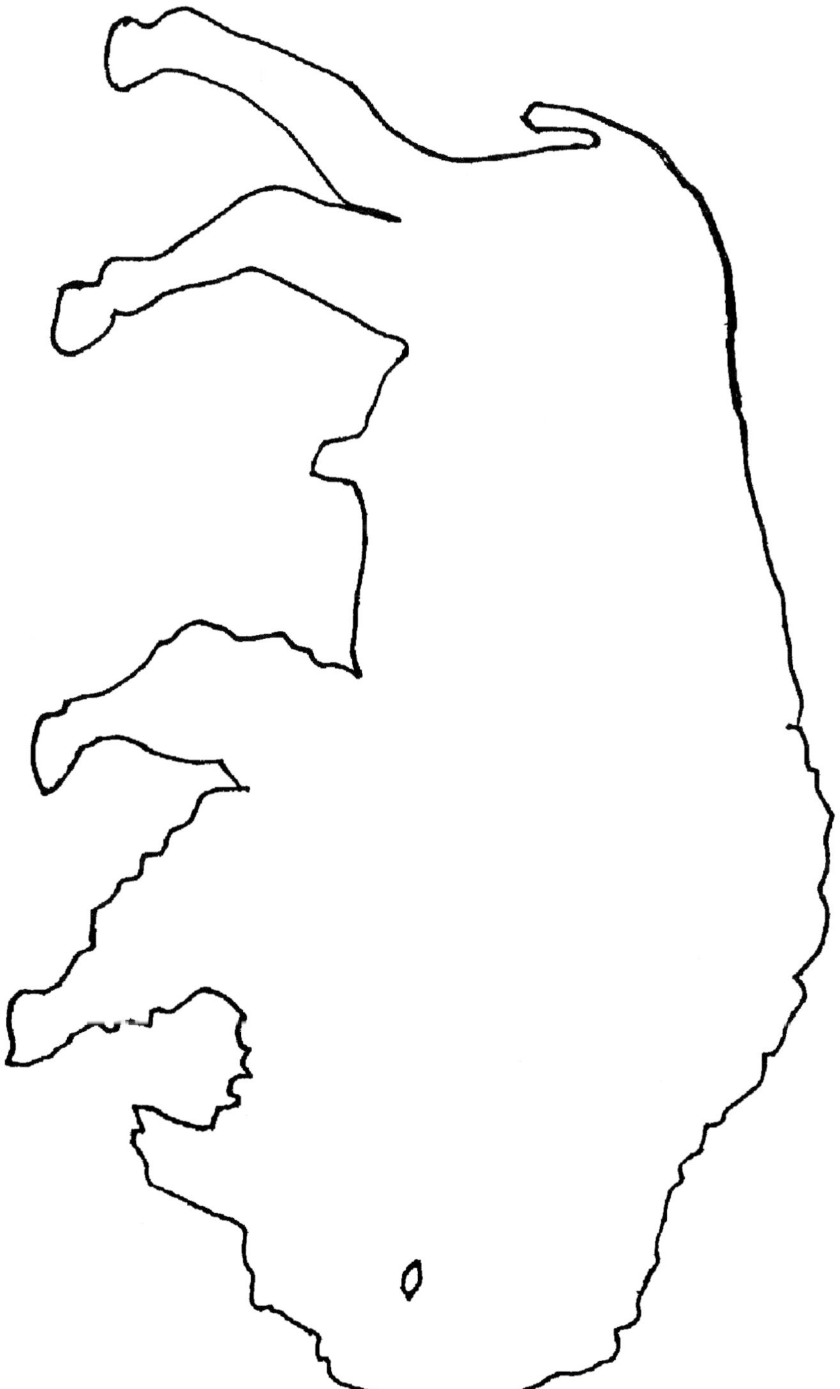

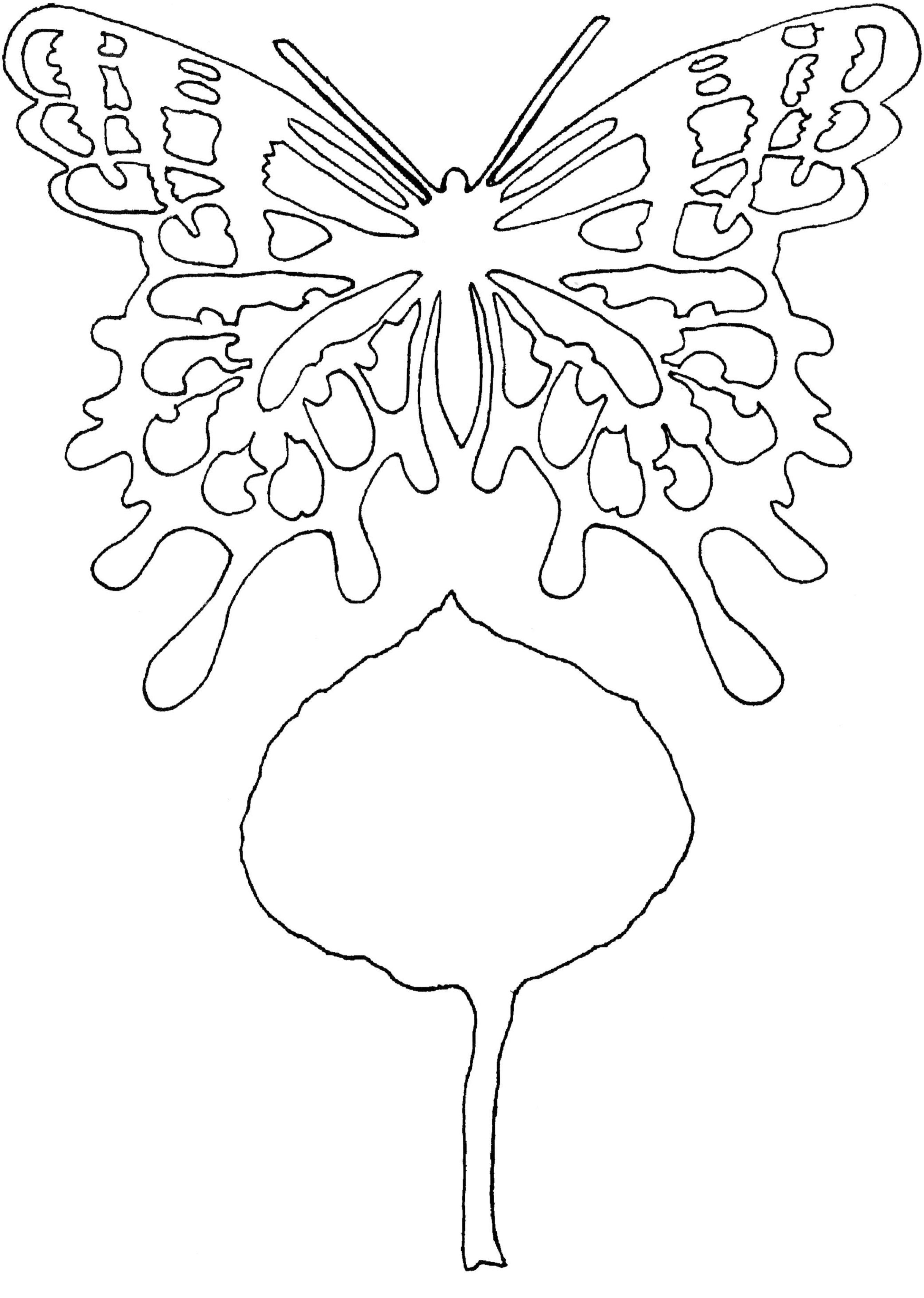

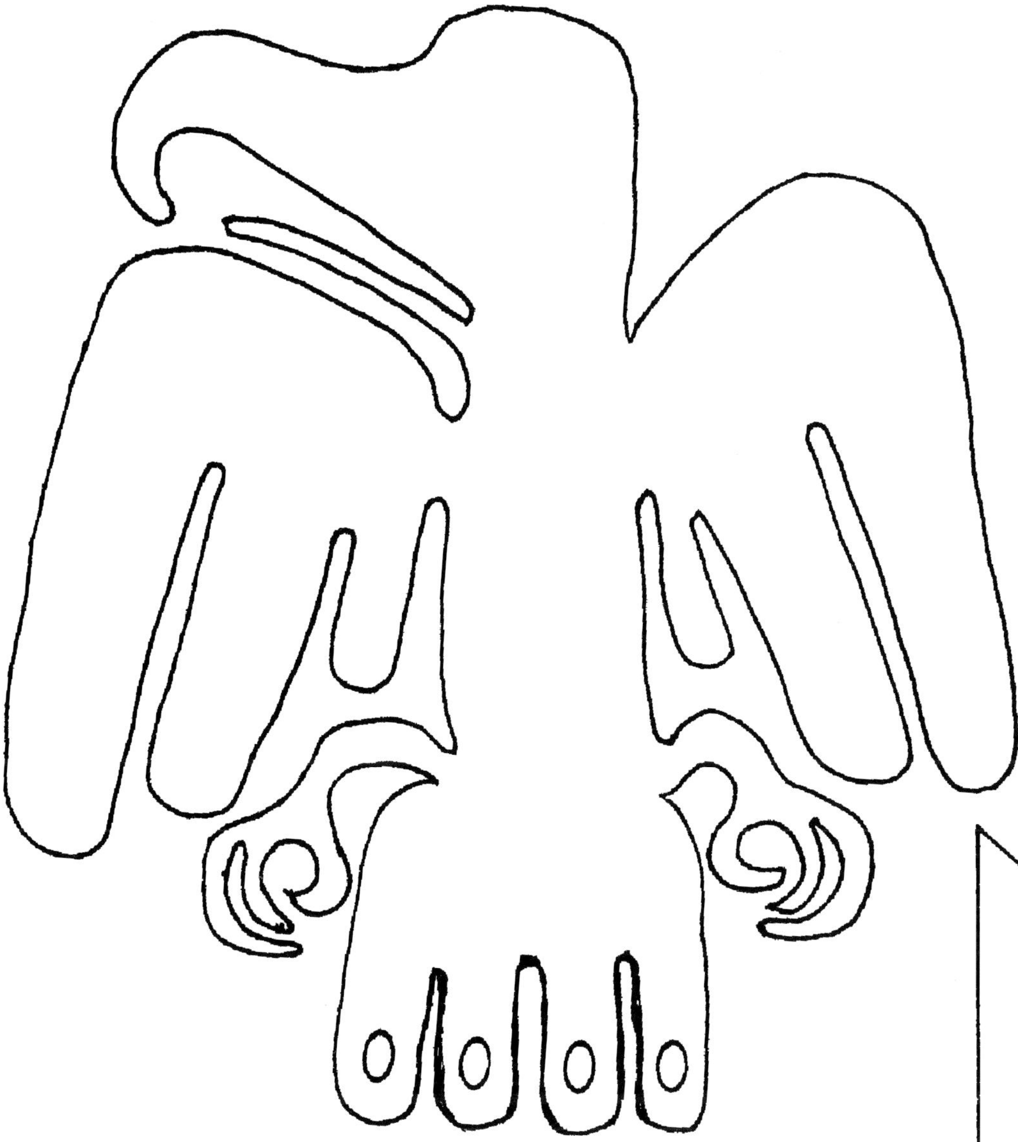

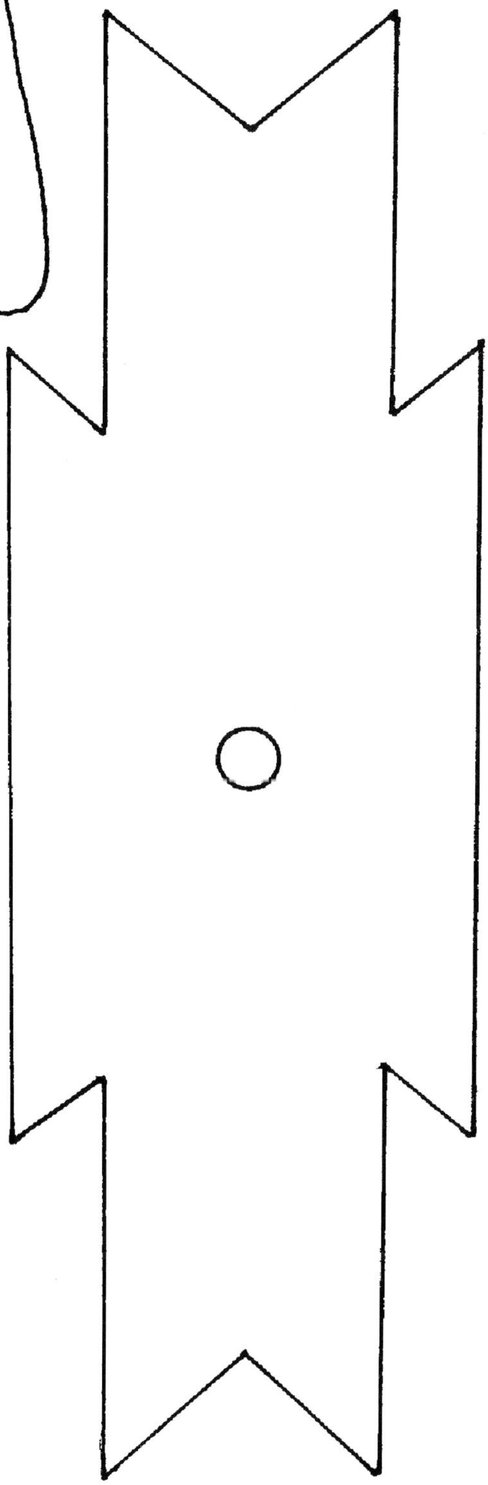

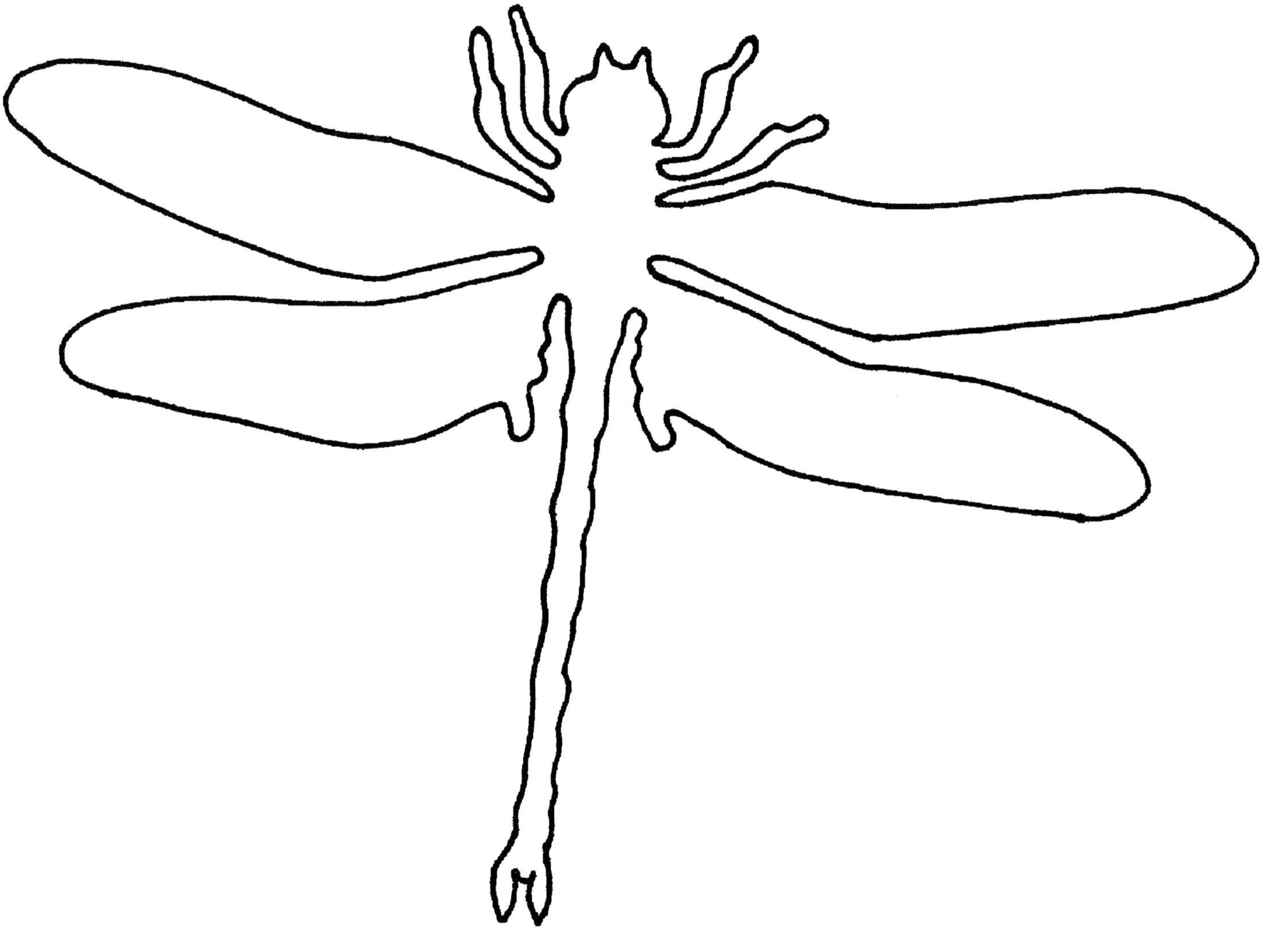

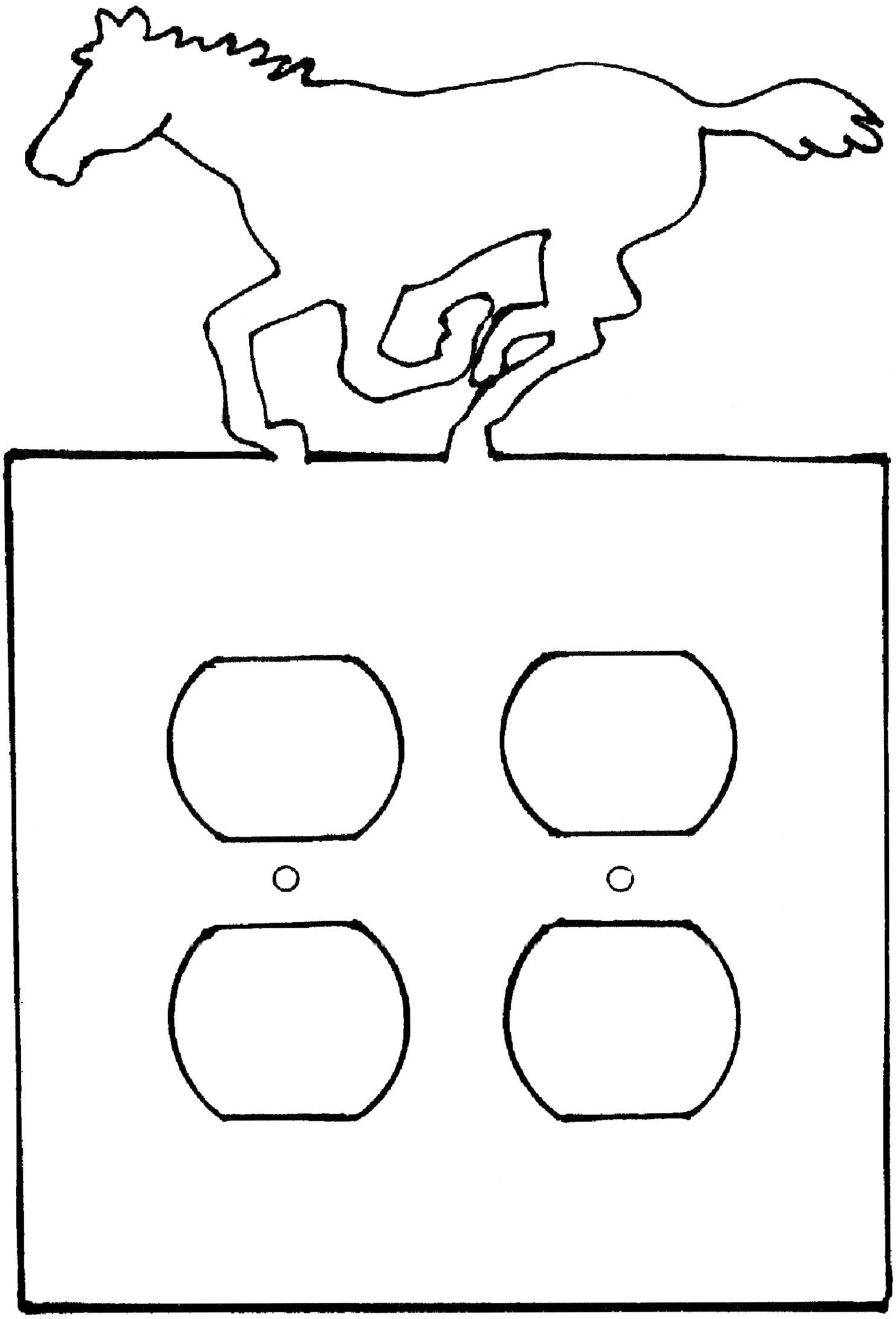

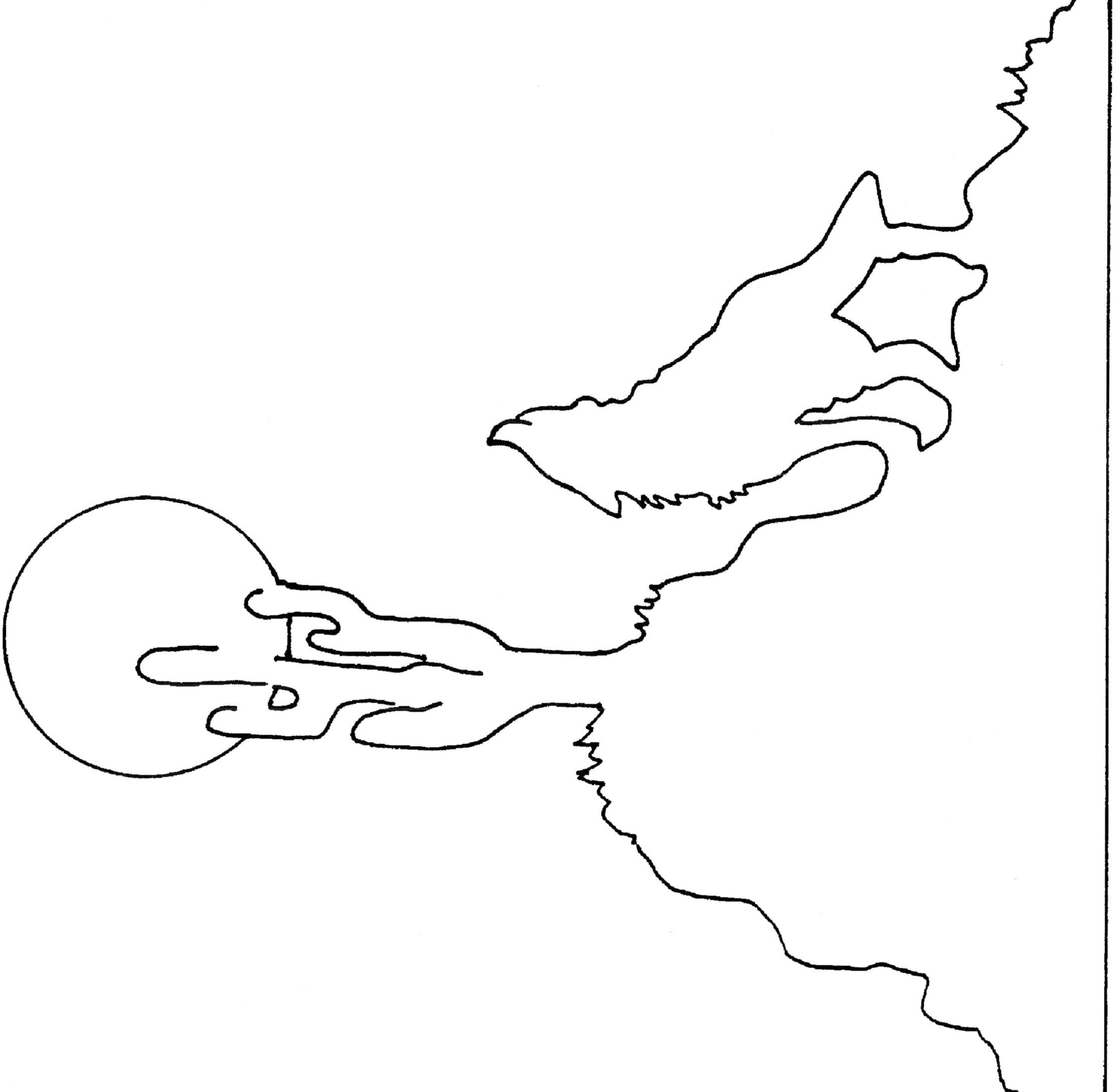

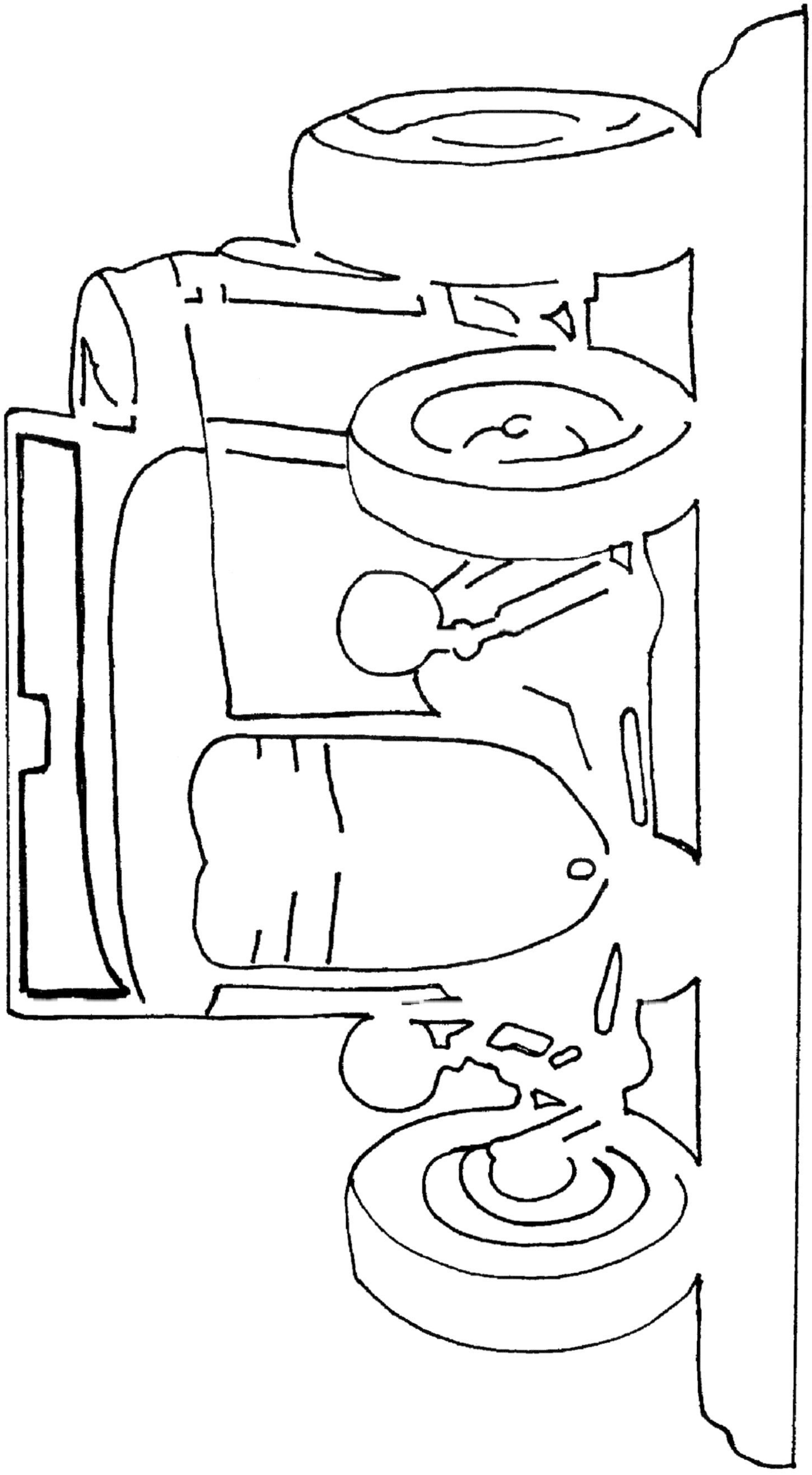

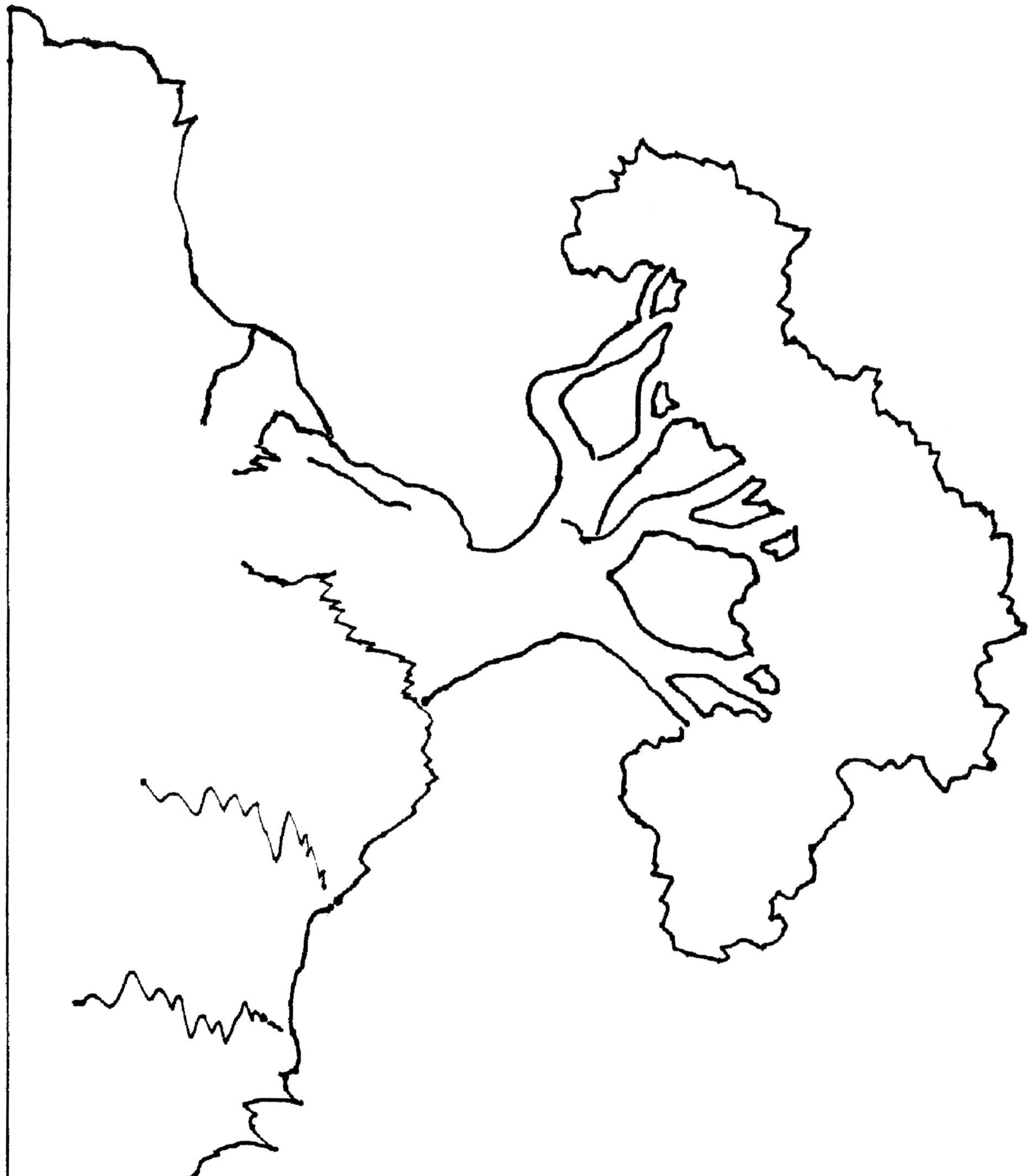

USA

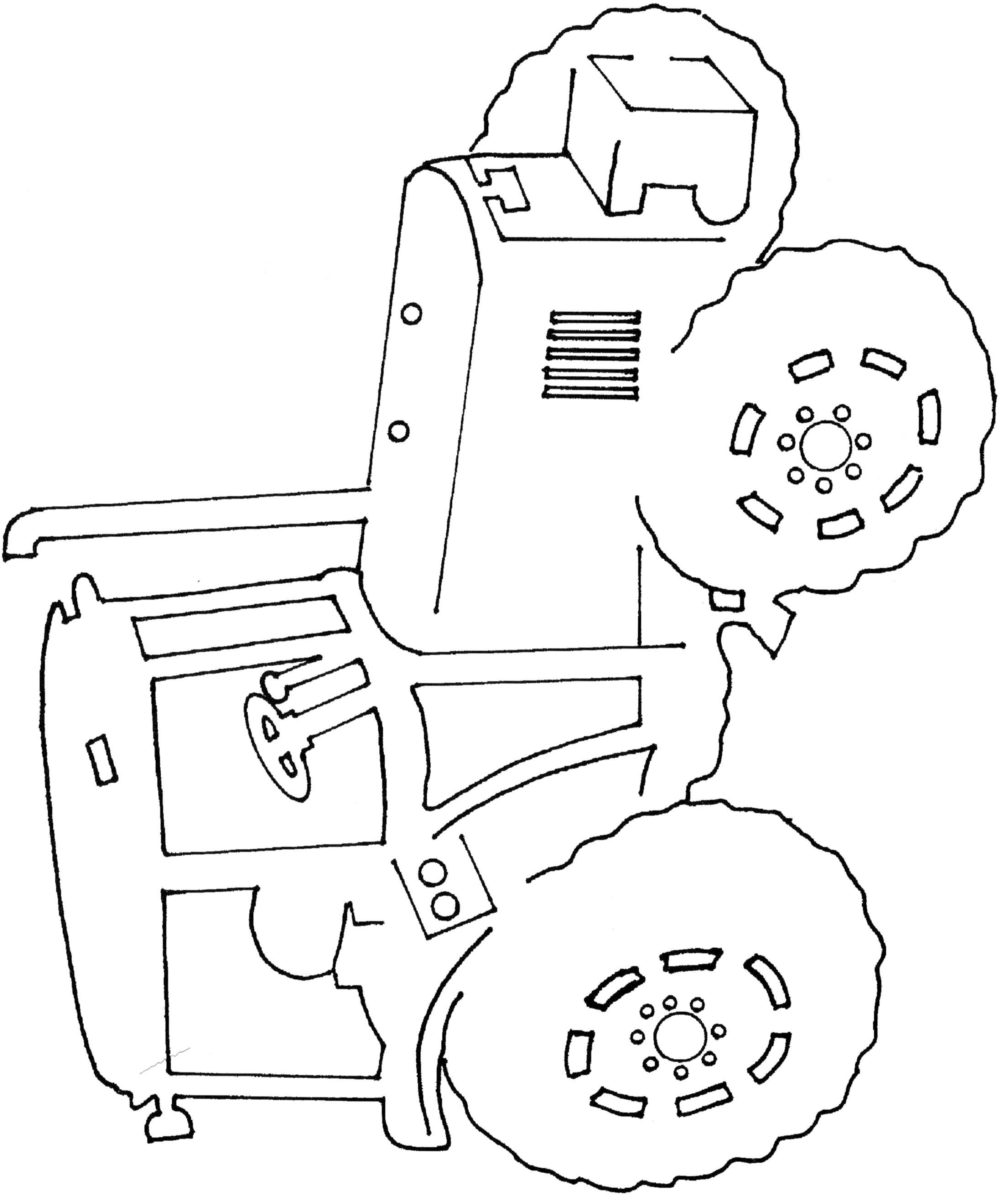

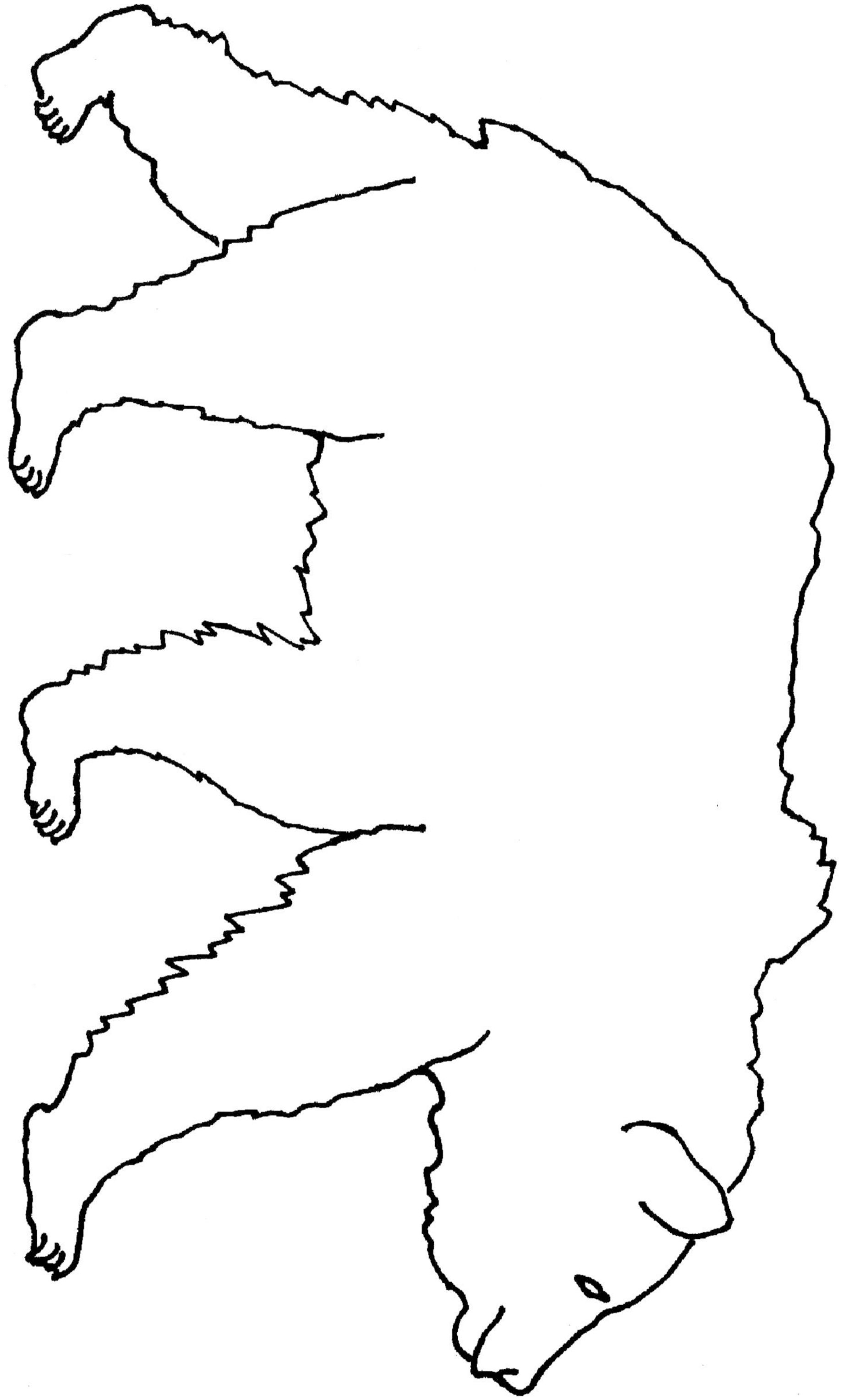